THE EXCESSES THE CAPRICES

PHILLIP FOSS

LIGHT AND DUST BOOKS

1991

ISBN 0-87924-076-8

Cover painting "Heart of Darkness,"
oil on canvas, 72" x 58", by Mark Spencer,
represented by Sena Galleries, Santa Fe.
Cover design by Mark Spencer.

Printed on recycled paper.
Manufactured in the U.S.A.

Light and Dust Books
Membrane Press
P.O. Box 4190
Kenosha, Wisconsin 53141

CONTENTS:

Acknowledgements:

Thanks to the editors of the following publications in which some of these poems first appeared:

Conjunctions: TH'EXCESS OF GLORY OBSCURED; As when the Sun new-ris'n looks through the Horizontal misty Air shorn of his Beams

Hambone: Musician of Fallacy
                Contempt Cloth

Notus: The Usual
                Prescriptive Equinox

o·blɐ̃k   The Elegant Predations
                The Painted Windows

Taos Review   Magic of Contagion

Tyuonyi: Hummingbird Cata

The title, "Th'excess of Glory Obscured . . ." is from Milton's *Paradise Lost*.

For my parents

NORTH HEAVEN

Scudding clouds   so mountains are gone
The feast is of air   before the conversant season
while distortion is attributed   to dialect
The choice of accompanying gesture   is oneiric
consistently inappropriate   thus compelling
solitude   and cognition of disappearance
There is no sensation   to accompany this
so one is contrived   or elicited
from flesh   to fix a sense of measure
So many fantasies   about value but oblivious
to seasonal melting   Thus days
become vignettes   cluttered with common displays
and the talent is not mesmerizing   but fatiguing
so solace is sought in hallucination and random construction
contradicts the gift of bruised milk

Again inclemency   is an attitude
and the compatible ascending chord   in praise
is merely distraction   making weather humane
With the collapsing refrain   halls are antiquated
as a matter of taste   or tribute to an imagined romance
and spaciousness mutates   to flux
or a geometric corner   where altitude is confined
to horizon   with predicated sea
This is post-hope   a state of redundance
and collusion   where boat-tailed birds
are fixed in flight   to adumbrate what they are not
thus subdued to ease   and the tenacity
of painted flight or plummeting

Remembered image is exact   yet the present
image more satisfying   This prevents succumbing
to death like desiring   spaces
between plants in a landscape   dominated by space
Thus white summer dresses   and inability
to come to consciousness   a kind of mystical entrapment
wherein the unimagined   flesh is equally doubted
because there is never rest   and again the sun
rises, a patient mistake   This is fabricated history
the phantom riding   over the hill
bereft of memory   and innocent of theatrics

Not participating in theatrics   makes winter exact
Silence, as linearity   remains cohesive
preventing closure   so there is no audience
to sanctify   or another silence to elicit
What remains is a redolent continuity   time
in torture   being relative, or water
whisked against gravity   New passion
is thus subversive   and the odor of juniper the cognate
around which the world is structured   Or anything else
Thus eagerness compels participation   in anonymity

Then it is all hoax
like having suspended
or the way an insect mars water
of transgression, the small
which is ants. The mundane
or its shadow
Superficial disassociation
the orchestration litter
the response is like instruments
complacency or condition empathetic
or the grotesques
postured as though dead
fluttering at the imagined deception

what marries the horizon
the idea of rejoice
Such is critical
puddle of blood
pops in and out like a puppet
against the greater landscape, mundane
is dismemberment
So when called like dogs
a preverbal
with cloud shadows
on the lawn
their small hearts

So what is confirmed?
of traduction
voice slathers
but in contagion
to itself in minimal exhaltation
its mountains gone
with suffering numerology
where each animate hope
so much rot
of plant and planet
to flight or an antiquated notion
Can tesselation then occur
from the insemination

That the eye is the vehicle
That the coquettish
That there is no respite
Or the year confined
its clouds scudding
into fading and relic
and nostalgia
collapses into itself
and the esteemed hierarchy
is discarded as impediment
of seduction
to and fro
of desire, chance stars

EVOLUTION OF DELIGHT

> Sexuality and death are simply the culminating
> points of the holiday . . . G. Bataille

This is night.

There is a category of intent related to sleep;
the affinities being subsumed under descent.

Sepia is a decline into antiquation: the faces
appear to organize a genetics since dissipated.

Perhaps war or a genetics associated with mines.

The way silver is in veins.

Blue glass discarded near collapsed mines:
when one peers through, one is beneath water.

And beneath sky.

Blue is related to black.

As the redundancy of closing one's eyes in darkness.

A cellar.

Inevitably there is a pile of coal.

Or a winery and the comfortable absence of light
so as not to disrupt mutation.

And associated drunkenness, like a boat
slowly sinking into a still lake at night.

Or drowning in an aquifer and being simultaneously buried.

The vagina as sleep, or alcohol.

To sleep in a house of ice with open eyes
and believe the glimpsed stars are beneath water.

2

There is a corpse drifting with currents
below the ice.

Its lips are red with burgundy.

The sun is eclipsed.

There are dancers on the ice
singing into tortoise shells.

Their rhythmic steps do not alter the currents.

The corpse is drifting in a house of ice.

The sun looks like a silver ring on its finger,
or its eye.

They are not singing about the sun but are stretching
the season like blown glass.

The corpse can hear them singing, but imagines
their words as its thoughts.

It is snowing and the dancers try to inhale
the flakes in order to drown.

The flakes melt on their open eyes and affect tears.

The tears in the corpse's eyes are salt
and taste like sweat on the dancers' backs.

Their naked torsos are shiny as if they had just broken
up through the ice.

They see the corpse through the ice and believe it
to be the season refracted, like glass, into elongation.

3

She believes she is inside her.

Then will she be her: a platinum eggshell;
or is she then only participating in parasitism:
a platinum diffusion.

She observes her hands distorting beneath water;
the veins are silver; she could fashion earrings.

She can see the reflection of her lips; they are red
with oxygen, but she is not breathing.

She sees the other's memory in sepia;
it is not her memory also, though she is inside her,
as in a tortoise shell.

She cannot see, except memory, so what occurs
cannot be other than as fed through the other's memory,
lapsed,

like allowing one end of the spectrum, broken
through a prism, into one's mouth.

4

He wonders if his head could be reinserted,
as one would stuff the bloody body
of a tortoise back into its shell.

□

PRESCRIPTIVE EQUINOX

                                        Red veins in green,
to console   such demarcation of placement;
interception in identification.

                                        Grammatical affection
or the glassed dog   are obtrusive in deference
to memory of an imagined emotion, felt.

            Because purple flowers littering the world.

Seduction of smell   where trees bleed,
truncated cloud or a bed of brush.

                    Passive flow of which the body calls akin
in refrain or mirror.

                                So servile lips engender fear,
an insomnia of animals,   laziness in departing mountains.

Brown reflects yellow, a condition of interiority.

                                One raven and the tendency to build;
or to drift   over the line
a collective exclamation.

            Then it is autumn like clothing or blue glass.

In Chinese, a colorful life, or the roof is red.

                                        Windmill is fatigue;
composite of shed hair and adrenaline.

                                        Smoke affronts strolling,
some collusion of opposites   and uses of air
or a wagon-load of pumpkins.

            Illiterates require graphics, not the thirsty breasts.

Now in drinking one becomes prey.

                                The churches twin each other
but are antonyms   when considered seasonally.

Falling leaves, brown river, one swallow.

   The occupying forces are corpses, some not even memory.

Chain is metaphorically related to white quartz, only.

                    A program of sunflower subsumed under lava.

Being corrupted by juniper   or the dwarf
where drunks are killed   and birds stomp tin roofs.

Thus absence of a vehicle for consensus.

                              Marigolds posited as stone.

Topography of pepper   where the elusive station
is described as portrayal of spiders.

                    A quotation evolved through amnesia
or the courtesan   a figment.

Often stones remain unmoved by human intervention.

                              Fluids to alter chemistry
through removal,   or the dead musician
creating a fuss.

                              Accident, thus disarmed
through fluency   and redundance of motifs
purported to mimic the sacred.

          The yellow melon and white squash watched
against inclemency   or the neighbor
in death by subtraction.

                    Some children become raptors
by upbringing, or sewage   converts to depression.

Given the fat   there is sufficient
intercourse and, maligned,   confluence is diverted
to reason.

The condition of the moon
in response to responsive culture   where the watcher
appropriates rock   to calendar vocabulary.

Explosive fruit responds to heat like notation.

        Bloody arms are predicated in the pursuit of comfort.

The question of knives   produces irritation
due to the appearance of pinions   and identity.

Thus the quirt is seasonal determinism,   a position
of descent antecedent to yellow.

☐

THE ELEGANT PREDATIONS

The nausea of lilacs: a preverbal vertigo or incandescent gesture such that voice disintegrates into a cosmology of animals and instruments. Is she then frightening? Is she then a horse or violin? Perhaps near enough to smell her breath her irises will expand horizontally. Or perhaps there is a red snake tattooed between her buttocks curling up her spine. Then the interiors of her pores will have the fragrance of lilacs.

Teeth do not shine in the absence of light. Thus it is
pointless to sift through loam at night, even if your
wrists are fatigued from conducting the flight of birds.
And she might have a small bird in her mouth, in place
of a tongue. Or a child's tooth as a fingernail, the
strength of which would be in implied threat.

The intent is to create a church of sound, a baroque vehicle
for image, and these a sonata of bastard symbols: a crown of
smoky quartz, a silver stirrup, or a whale's pelvis; a
foundation of pure projection, not unlike a voice creating
three notes at once. Thus succumbing to an animism disguised
by artifacts of desire, like red.

This could be the endless recitation of texts to prevent
erosion of civilization, as if sounds were not merely
mnemonic devices for thought, but brief projectiles
refracting off what is imagined to be divisive to continuity:
finding a marble inside a hen's egg, or combing a tarantula
from one's hair. Such are exaltations of device: a clock
work which turns in the head as an amateur impersonation of
physics.

Extensions of the body clutter the scenery: looms and
revolvers waiting for fingers to prompt articulations
of which the fingers alone are incapable. A lie would
be appropriate now: an adamant proclamation about the
temperature of crystals when invited to heal a dislocated
personality: that assumed when one is discovered sucking
nectar from flowers.

Or to quarrel with physicians about the color of your eyes
and, lacking a mirror, or not believing in mirrors, you are
always correct and allowed to change your claim at will.
Thus to subvert the finality of naming, disallowing anything
to gell or reach maturity, like iridescent fish eating their
offspring a second after birth: it is that instant when the
mimes leap on stage and fail with one collective gesture.

The pictorial histories carved in stone are all fabrications, not designed as temporal refutations, or false scent-trails, but glorifications of failed memories, or comets. Perhaps they are sufficient to die for, as good as wheat fields hosting hallucinogens, or a breastful of photographs of individuals assumed to have lived, their tongues uniformly drooping like limp fish.

What is desired is the recollection of odors, perhaps a
theater of odors which compels a mental seasickness from
the movement of its waves; as the gull flies upside down,
confident the sea will not turn to rain. Or the tongue up
the neck where acidity refutes the romance of the nose. And
the red peels off the lips and the hair is thrown on the
floor, like a taxidermist's experiment.

The trees change color so rapidly you lose all sense of
direction and believe that by sitting still the flocks of
cranes plodding toward you will not discover the roses
you are hiding inside your shirt: you wish to create a
language that is pure red, and you wish to speak it on
a day of pure snow.

You can visualize what you wish to speak: the red and orange
sunset, the finger-wide band of erect pubic hair visible
through her pink gown, and darkness reeking of lilac. But
you are afraid because you understand that each tone
corresponds to a hue. Thus even in darkness you could
create a cacophony, like the decomposition of fireworks
or the dissection of desire.

□

AESTHETIC OF POVERTY

The collection had mutated

It was recalled as countries   but had become paper
Not lanterns   yet related to light
like Halloween   The faces smiling and drunk
giving away what rain   had collected in their palms
at night   spit or blood

The pieces were too small   to fold into representations
of something they were not   a boat
or death's head tattoo   graceful causality

Or a bird   could be identified
incorrectly because countries   though adjacent
have no dialectical lineage

                          This would not apply to women
although cadence was antithetical   to sharing nostalgia
Thus lanterns   are dead people
or insect traps

                                 Painted topographies
like rouge and tears   the same story about autumn
and fish inflated with drought Only in capillaries of shade
is there reduction of the body

                                 So the season is named
prematurely or latently   with affection and teeth
in the light-burning wood   where oblique darkness
creates the usual despair   of duality

Some say this results from entertaining distracting thoughts
refusing to accept   a rotting ship
as allegory   though motion is implicit and water
beneficent to any confession   be it retribution
or benign response

                International memory is then discarded
like paper or planets   This is a chaste
rejection   one wherein the fragrance lingers
as invitation   or gagging
is suspended decorously

thus anonymous
in to fill character, cloud
eyes roam peripherally
trying to observe scent

Faces are always racially specific
where lips suck an imagined word
or intoxicated
for evasion
rejecting proximity

Then one memorizes species of pine
other than heat or paper
of course, is age. So
in turning like chorus
in falling

to what end
and the semblance one has
the sheets are observed
or hope

One could conclude that battles
coincide with the notion of vogue
and the world young
its shadows swinging gently

facing wind
a day resolved before dawn
in gradations of repose

The challenge is
to whatever pictured rivers
in taste
the issue in a monologue
for air
paper is exclusion
an illicit desire

to assign confluence
one has confirmed
Spaciousness is not
composed of synonyms
though the way fingertips touch
like the inability to walk

or the delicate hand
and the lacquered hand

with lacquered nails
the delicate nails

THE USUAL

and the season a projectile.

                             threats from the lord

with bright fruit
in conversion, and trees

                                 Not angst but ax
                             inflating mouths
falling toward mnemonics.

Nothing but deceit:
contradictions: four stalks of grass
of snow, and the enemy love complacent.

to tesselate the grotesque
                             bandage

                                 Old age

sickness, disease, death
said to swirl:
but in ten faces
and earth outside sinking.

and the beautiful
                               this is an octet
with the words rhyming

counting out syllables
the seasons to redundance.

                             Now it is a hammer
                               to accelerate

It is necessary to amass numerous,
horoscopes as excuses
the equilibrium of fog.

                             preferably false,
for failing to confront

This is finally a question
and how one eviscerates

of tilth
music through suction.

That the old snow appears
                             is insufficient

as a wall
for the derivative meditations

and dismemberments

The fluttering water
like the date,

                             and icy bridge are,
arbitrary divisions

of light.

and the prehistoric corn

                                        Resigned to drought
                                  divisive toward appetite.

So the woman is bitter   about aduration and atonality.

The refuse of living is stuff.

                                        Adolescent causality:
frost and shadow.

                        The mind inconsistently inappropriate
to the body   and other amputations.

Passing over a quick death is obvious.

                                Failing to accept any premise
creates-a-somnolent-inventory.

                        Or, having failed to acquire any proximity
to continuity,   white clay deposits
or tactility of snow.

The black painting   or the pants
are splashed with blood: the options coalesce
in the intrusive voice.

                                There is this constant laughter
like mephistophelian ridicule   and the dog
is intentionally strangling itself.

                                The stonework is molecular
but its image is slavery: either condition finite
like illusive clouds.

Eating the cactus buds
produces an archaic sensation the eyes itch.

As such is causality radical
and the blank wall a star map?

□

CONTEMPT CLOTH

So it all gets away
back in a false archaeology
in a repudiation
becoming canvas
resembles a vulva
or lack of meaning
of givens
and a refusal of particulars
So failed hostilities
against those articulated with little memory
or neglect
more or less

The collected artifacts broadcast
beloved weapons
or visual memory
The wounded tree
because warmth of the spring sun
has contributed to this confusion
Escape is into spaciousness
or ease of falling
are reconciled
of origin
and blood evaporates

What is centrifugal
the elaborate growing
but a maxim
that *is* joyous
So too there is the winsome
of roses
and the sensation of speed
or the whole notion
Thus there is communication
more adept than intrusion
to collapsing perception
toward dearticulation
removing a particular from its place

is attributed to ease
not a condition
like the failed fire of the river
not in fallacy but declaration
eternal drudgery
with the sky escaping above
decidedly incorrect
needing dispensation
of quivering
of sound in response
as song moves
each utterance

The orchestration is vindictive
only one side of the face
of mood
and lights extractions
of leakage
without even the rudiments
As also with protestation
beyond vibration

a way of burning
to create a juxtaposition
Or night a series of glossy walls
or, at least, points
where what had been desired escapes
of memory
the reeds water-logged
and fingers retarded with season

bearing the relativity
or spontaneity of north
is then affected
of fore and aft
what emotion being overlaid

Having the oblique pain
like magnetics
is reoriented away from consensus
as absent
and thus unthinkable
against passivity
which mimics debilitation
to the speaker's posture
of collusion
like the imagined music
or perception
the difference in temperature between two sides of a wall
as a mental aid
where the-misperceived
toward what is declared
from any lexicon
provides a hysteria
like the random slur
and calls attention
creating the impression
between sound and form
accompanying a wounded animal
without consciousness:

Becoming a refutation
where the hand
not in violence
or the child correctly
of a planet
of a garden
the mosaic of nuance
or fall
by chance or intent
reappropriated in a manner
and thus repulsive
of the fabrication collapse
synonymous with what surrounds it
of empiricism
does go through the wall
but molecular empathy
mispronounces the name
to destabilize the artifice
Such imposition becomes scattered message
lost as in a delirium
where the pieces are misshapen
and the initial composition
which is strange
making the desire
into an anonymity

HUMMINGBIRD CATA

The jaw does not open; the manners of sleep. Or the impinging
white of mountains. This is a mansion of refuse, ants
tenacious as boredom, and the seasonal optic a pornography
of health. The black hair to her knees, a tunnel? Overture,
to overthrow, a strophe or merely a door, no cajoling light
within. Gifts as from clouds, nameless, or reticent, the
invading decline a burn and limp. Or excellent candles
feigning interrogation and the surrounding night a purse,
as sex, or flowers voluptuous in moonlight. The textiles of
rumination are a dearticulated rainbow richoceting light
with random collusion, and smoke proposed as a symptom of
milk, the interstice, perhaps, vapor. To achieve this tension,
and arrive at arbitrary notes, is music or weaving or archery:
to propel.

The symptoms are interminable speech, like clover, or growth,
the condition exasperated by hair confronting. Doors open,
revealing sustenance or drainage, the aria a mere slamming,
and edifices of delight, repositories of urine; like the sun
destroying a wardrobe without record of contempt. As to
complete a barn, one must die, not in causality, but as
monument to stasis. The tossed stone remained for ten
thousand years unturned, then nothing. To select by what
then? The numerology of wood grain, like curtains? The
professed remembrance of dance? Or breasts as surrogates of delight?

To assemble is to draw Xs across the eyes of the assembled,
stone or entropy, the margin in another nationality or hope.
Continuous acceleration precludes the view, no sense in the
divisive, like rapt wonderment at teeth: the impossible.
Collect the tokens, be they tangible or sentiment, as badges
to shoreup against the invincible de-. Or martyr all manner
of sufferages, the spring wind or profusion of skies. To
move sand from one location to another creates an other at
both: or at least trespass, like blinding, and releasing, a
bird to infer nuances of gravity.

Or to believe in the illusion of mobility like the vertigo
caused by a snake roaring is to throw the designed juxtaposition
askance, as dropping one wing of a butterfly two millimeters
causes it to fly in circles. Then it is the gravity of
retrogression, like a child falling down, falling down, falling
down, falling down, and the wind returning north. Or sitting
in the dirt peering into a crystal and seeing the devil. How
many sopranos to shatter? Or to collect the collective hate
and hold it in your palm like a small desire or animal. Can
one then acrobat the ecstatic music with the projected
duality of a magpie or obliterate all memory in the cause
of pleasure?

To design the world through erosion, the way bass notes are
a finger plucking another instrument in your ribs, is the
same as the old man who has been grubbing out the same weeds
on the same wisp of soil for ten thousand years, stopping
periodically to eye the weather and change his face. Does the
sky finally possess his redundance, like a limitless string
of paper dolls flapping up in ascension? Can you then convert
to a sensate and run your tongue up the crack in the ground
as an apology for the past? Or recite the names of the clouds
blindfolded using sign language, thus creating layers of
non-cognition and still believe it a form of asympathetic
magic? But all causality is random: a domino theory of chance,
where a dragonfly directs the movement of fire through a
village.

□

ENJOYING TO FORGET

Because the view   alludes to personal declination
goat hair   is posited as erectiles
and body hair   assumes a bestial aptitude:
one man in death   with conversance.

This is assumed through misanthropy   but soil is blue
with birds   circumnavigating his home
or perhaps a mental   disorder wherein the symbols
no longer represent sounds: thus that we become mute
and the inarticulate thrives: an arm through the brain.

Not a metaphor   but visualization:
the man is abbreviated: one sound.

So desert   is an annoying excess
because failure is perceived as a liquid,   causing altitude
to be perceived as divine.

Descending pressure   and the trivial mystical enough
to forestall conversion   to star eye.
Snow is orthodox.

Are green walls then fecundant   and the text submissive
to gravity   so that in conjunction
it is despairing to alter?   Or that covetous birds
enact a refutation of temperature?

Mute equations   and music is inarticulate
beyond an irritation in the bones.

Personal names   to refresh the provided,
like new stars or a dog.   There is the webbing,
repeatedly, the webbing to question.

A cosmology of marks;   reductivism, but sufficient
for passion and interest: or: a tesselation of the elements
of consciousness with no   controlling factor:
clouds or hate for instance: is cosmos, with leaves.

Suffering to reinstate the bland color,   like walking
on irregular ice,   concentration
obscures the personality,   and excuses
for living are dearticulated.

Hilarity is converted   to humus, its echoic
predilection abandoned in cognition of planetary conjunction
Thus planting and lust   are condoned
in submission to the character   of light.
This too has been abandoned.

What is hidden   beneath snow does not exist.
Besides, it is a cacophony   and one
becomes disturbed at failing   to discover dead birds.
They have been erased   through a wonder sufficient
to forget everything,   or are merely lost.

THE PAINTED WINDOWS

Through the empty arch comes an air of the mind that blows
insistently over the heads of the dead . . .
Federico Garcia Lorca

As if a conspiracy
to refute reflection
or condoning
      of polished
interiority:
     the landscape
inside a vase;
a house glazed blue:
the erection
      of an eye,
that of a dragonfly;
 or a darning needle
postured between
       fingers
as echoic
    of a cigarette.
And, like goggles,
  hands are cupped
over the eyes,
    palms tattooed
with goldfish,
      to imitate
silk.
     And the child
in the crib,
    singing chords
like a player piano,
is a ventriloquist's
dummy.

The wall said,
          "redemption",
causally introducing
          the saxophone
as an equation
  against the implied
coy: the wall
          has no window
other than as mouth
              for voice,
as such is painted
  with the landscape
projected beyond it.
    Yet, those walking
do not walk:
              a portrait
of death;
like singing of love
to a skull;
              the desire
to animate
  would participate
in animism:
    perceiving thighs
as repositories
    of bones capable
of fabrication
              into flutes:
sex.

The windows
          are black:
soot, darkness,
      blindness, sleep,
paint: fire,
          the division
of light,
          lost gnosis,
the coma,
                white.
The panes of glass
   burning in the fire
give off
          an inversion
of light
      in which the skin
of the hands
      can be removed,
like gloves.
          Such behavior
is predicated
          on analysing
the dreams
      of the oversoul;
in the same way
          one can float
down a river
on the inflated skin
of a pig.

Windows of the soul,
          thus painted
in prostitution,
     perform a theater
of introspection,
            wherein lust
is a handmirror
        gloved in a wig:
a dionysian waltz
        executed bereft
of audience;
          the wine bottle
a magnifying glass
which, when looked
through, straightens
              the world
from its convexity.
          The *duende*
of the genitals
jumps up and down
with malice.

Suicide is then
   a critique of time,
as a mime's face
         is a critique
of immortality:
         how disease
and winter
         form a satyr,
their conversation
                  braille
written with frost
         on a window.
Thus in touch
perhaps tenderness,
is dissolution
         and the view
is rectified,
       not telescoping
into limpidity
or ocular profundity
but, like myopia,
the pane is cracked
by the invention
       of the forehead:
a crypt
       in which to seat
a bullet: idol.

□

THE MAGIC OF CONTAGION

                The site of consciousness
is the unpainted decoy. A raven dies in flight: three
colors: red, black, blue.

            He can move the ivory and ebony
chess pieces by concentrating on his fingers through the
decoy's eyes. His fingers feel botanical. His eyes are painted
blue; the ink smells of old garments.

               He can open his eyes in the
glass reflection. They are glass; a membrane binds them to
an aquatic diffusion.

              He can hear the music of his
heart deteriorating. It is contrived, of wood. It is beneath
the boards beneath his feet. Thieves. He wishes to model it.

              He is in a window. It is winter.
His tongue tastes of brass. He wishes to speak. His words are
in his palm: bone dice inscribed with Roman numerals.

            He remembers there is a door
in his chest; he imagines a theater performs, thus the sound
of his heart is not deterioration, but soliloquy. Opera.

              He is singing. It is night. His
voice is breaking windows. It has legs and kicks
with satisfying violence. The fragments he renames windchimes
and feels them as his fingernails when they click together.

              He is in a tree. It is summer.
His mouth is full of revolver cartridges. He assumes these
are his teeth, inscribed with aliases. When he swallows them
he is afraid he is slowly becoming old.

He is in a tree. It is winter.
The decoy is a raven. It wishes to speak but its glass eyes
have inverted him so that he is hanging by his feet.

He is peering through many panes
of glass. He is able to throw his voice into their interstices;
and each voice is from an age in his past. He calls to them,
and they answer, with nicknames.

He is peering through many panes
of glass. Each is coated with a layer of frost. In their
interstices are images of himself from his past. With the chess
pieces and the dice he can rearrange the images and thus avoid
condemnation.

The site of his consciousness
is a pane of glass. Since it is a liquid he assumes he can
flow. But its rate of movement is so minuscule he ceases to
think.

He is playing the violin. The
site of consciousness is his hands. His hands believe it
is a woman; the skin vibrating beneath his fingers. The violin
sounds.

He is playing chess. He can
move the pieces without using his hands. He does not know
the rules. He is playing against no one. He understands that
the board is his back; the dark squares tattooed.

He is tattooing his eyelids in
the mirror. His eyes are shut. The tattoos are of his eyes. The
eyes of the decoy.

The eyes in the mirror are not
his eyes. They are blue and membranous. Thus he can observe
himself, a silhouette, with empathy.

He has cut out the silhouettes of
his profile as it has transformed since childhood. These are
his chess pieces. They are in a war over his back, yet are
all monochromatic.

He can project his voice into
each, but his sense of temporal linearity is oblique causing
the voice to be inappropriate, the baby cursing in sanskrit.

He wishes to destroy all the
caricatures of himself, to incinerate the puppets and dolls,
to have his numerous voices dissipate into star music.

He wishes to dissipate into
star music; to become an unnamed musical composition, one
which the body of a violin, a woman, could play without
the contagion of his consciousness.

☐

MUSICIAN OF FALLACY

The chance dissolution
beyond which is falling
into a language of soil
and dew, the way of seeing
is removed
To reach, then, the peculiar
not just as voice
against what falling
what has since been begun

to portraiture
a condition translated
like night singing
that what is moved
away from the love it has extended
vibration and hold it
but substance
is required to complete

Compelled to re-emote dread
or the way night is personified
-such is unction-
translucent laughter
interminably toward dissolution
of humor
what is disdained
plants, ubiquitous
bereft of hope

the tenor of a ruin
in displays of labor
the severe profile
plunging like refrain
This is the basic source
To cloak in black
and marvel at the green
flags of hope

Concerned to always be found   in this or other
season, a veil of rain   distorting the landscape
in which relics of persuasion remain   is perhaps
sleight of mind   as fragmenting voices
display emotions   curious, like birds
overcautious in wind   Some clarity
is nevertheless exuded   the notes of a violin
compel recrimination   the accent
adorably foreign   the vocabulary smoke

Such faith to appropriate sunlight   the gait is wrong
and the dalliance grotesque   The soil has
provokes, memory   The condition impedes upon itself
like flashing of cards   their artifice
wind sufficient to collect   the various sounds of death
Passage through air   is a nostalgia
a morning long refused   by dazzling light
altering the color   of knowing:
these clouds horribly mimic the music

Confess the solemn notation
Whistling late
What recourse but hair
the allure of semen
convulse trepidation
but ambiguities prosper
the cause of spasmodic articulation
of subliminal pornography
of impossibility

subterfuge of body
Spume of divinity
or sapphic drain:
Such repose is acute
a scar singular as signature
it is a foreign well
This is the recreation
words aping such positions

The calendar was ontic
a violent melody
like cats
being stationed
and roiled sea
originating at a different time and compel a liminal memory:
mummified hides
or posture as weapon
of sequence

thus hypocrisy
So the season is ubiquitous
Erasure is the ghost of possibility
between studded hill
The breeze carries odors
in a rotten loft
Thus the imagined memory
resembles the randomness of a flock

Discomposition   like the apparent tree
where the condition is articulated   through hue and tone
relieves what momentum   has dearticulated:
the will and spurious remarks   about the inevitable
Three blue-tailed lizards   are a syllogism
not a problem   and the attitude is predatory
conceived around levels of existence   not spirit
but strata   So the relegation is to a hierarchy
with the longer dead   not necessarily deeper or further

To telescope what has been compressed   through eroticism
and see the human   beleagured with visual mimicry
thus nameless   and a mere collection
is the fallacy   into which is fallen
As all landscape   is the mirage of desire
making the view two-dimensional   absent of texture
and journey   So topography is a graph
of lyricism, and mountains   are not echoic
but the caprice of collective seduction

That which is most dearly loved   is erosion
the eyes merely synonyms   of the lips
where gait is an exquisite   reproduction
of passion   and is squandered
Beyond good amusement there is but the critique of linearity
It all smells of being burned   like the coy
memories of what is loved   thrown over in a trough
of faces   so much debris
The song repeated   into a compaction of sterility

All that shall be   is a condition of rumination
like amnesia, the melody or horn section   and the poet
converted to autism   through acceleration
and spiritual repugnance   So with all aberration
the lights eventually go out   and the hands cease
to choreograph prayer   Layers of subterfuge
have previously been established   so the music proceedes
backward in a kind of personal   incest
without the accompanying mirror of water

☐

TH'EXCESS OF GLORY OBSCURED; As when the sun new-ris'n
looks through the Horizontal misty Air shorn of his Beams

The Equation

The dissonant intellect, like clarified percussion, cants

toward the oblique --a toxin obscuring the profile -- through

a species of interrogation which, though bloodless, reduces

the landscape to paper and motion to the purely ocular, like

a stylization of absent space: photographic renditions of

nudes. Thus recitation syncopates in monologue; a tremolo

of self-confirmation, redolent in masturbation, and the

plasticity of the body articulates with that of the view:

thus there is no disparity, but rather two mirrors wedded

in facing and the interstices, light.

It is a bandage for the eyes, a blindfold where resolution
is a pointillist matrix and the vibration expands like a
cloud of dragonflies.

The Articulation

Across some strait of intemperance -- or intolerance -- the

way yellow leaves cling to skin, is a device for insulation,

the consequences dismissed as fruits and the shadow of the

praying mantis a paradox of temptation. So there is no

equation: the rock is composed of smaller rocks but

repetition does not compose a melody, only another mirror

of consensus from which one must turn and refrain from

thought, the consequences of dissipation, or appropriate

garments of laughter -- like yellow leaves -- and assemble

the remnants immune to chaos or identity -- like shadows --

and weld some creature, a beatific scarecrow, to serve as

one's double, or shadow, and the avenue of impersonation

shall be in its gesture of indifference.

The sun does not move as a justification for seasons reminded
of discourse, nor the brain swell under the suspicion of
what the eyes may then recognize.

The Fabrication

The intervention of the body mutates the sound and the eyes
covet the image of flame and the flesh is glazed with a
window of ice. Condolences are offered; the view is obscured
by the eyes, the way fingers adhere to dry ice, as if in
longing: the great scripture of separation tattooed forever
into the tongue as a dismissal of speech. This then is
what is created: a labyrinth of dread where grotesques are
assembled in a circus of infallible theatrics and the
absence -- none of which is palatable -- and the light.

Consume the tired thoughts, the sluggish crawl toward
burrows of light as the dark birds sing freely to what
is colored.

(It all began as mere appetite.)